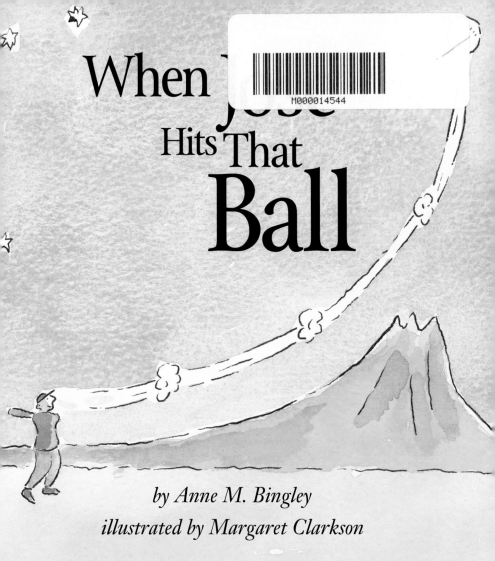

When Jose Hits That Ball

by Anne M. Bingley

illustrated by Margaret Clarkson

Learning Media®

When Jose hits that ball,
it flies …

over the wooden fence,

across the dry riverbed,

past the farmers' market,

between the rows of melons,

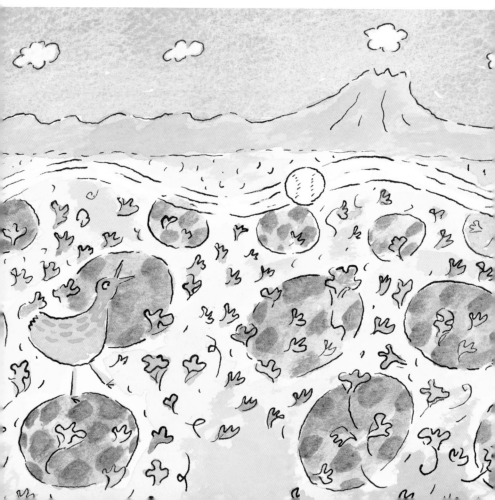

under the sign for Tio's Taquitos,

through Abuelita's laundry,

around the corner,

and back!

When Jose hits that ball ...

WE DUCK!